Walkies

DOG TRAINING AND CARE
the Woodhouse Way

BARBARA WOODHOUSE

ILLUSTRATIONS BY ANGUS SCOTT

SUMMIT BOOKS NEW YORK

Also by Barbara Woodhouse
NO BAD DOGS The Woodhouse Way

Originally published in Great Britain in 1982
by Ernest Benn Limited

SUMMIT BOOKS and colophon are trademarks of Simon & Schuster.

Designed by Martin Lee.

Printed in Spain by Artes Graficas Grijelmo, Bilbao.
ISBN 0-671-46892-8

CHOOSING YOUR DOG

YOU SHOULD ALWAYS CHOOSE THE BREED OF DOG YOU LIKE. ALL DOGS ARE NICE DOGS WHEN PROPERLY TRAINED.

THERE ARE ONE OR TWO THINGS TO BE CONSIDERED BEFORE YOU DECIDE ON YOUR DOG THOUGH. FOR INSTANCE, DON'T KEEP A LARGE DOG IN A TINY HOME. IT CANNOT HELP GETTING IN THE WAY.

THEN IF YOU HAVE LIMITED TIME TO BRUSH AND COMB YOUR DOG, DON'T CHOOSE A VERY LONG COATED DOG.

REMEMBER TOO THAT MOST TERRIERS NEED TRIMMING TWO OR THREE TIMES A YEAR. IF YOU HAVE TO PAY FOR THIS YOURSELF, IT MAY BE BETTER TO CHOOSE A SHORT-COATED DOG.

TRY TO FIND OUT WHAT THE BREED YOU CHOOSE IS REALLY MEANT TO BE KEPT FOR. IF YOU WANT A DOG FOR RATTING, DON'T KEEP A PEKINESE!

FINALLY, REMEMBER SMALL PUPPIES CAN GROW INTO BIG DOGS. IF YOU ARE BUYING A MONGREL, TRY AND FIND OUT WHAT ITS PARENTS WERE.

CARING FOR YOUR DOG

YOU WILL NEED TWO HINGES, A DOOR LATCH, ONE YARD OF FINE-MESH CHICKEN WIRE, SOME SCREWS, ONE-INCH NAILS AND A SAW. THE WIRE NETTING SHOULD BE PUT ON THE INSIDE OF THE DOOR TO KEEP THE DOG FROM BITING THE WOOD. BEWARE OF SHARP ENDS STICKING OUT. THE KENNEL SHOULD BE ON FIRM LOW LEGS.

ALL PUPPIES SHOULD HAVE AN INDOOR KENNEL WHEN THEY ARE SMALL AND BEFORE THEY ARE HOUSEBROKEN. FOR A SMALL DOG, THE CHEAPEST KIND IS MADE OUT OF AN ORANGE CRATE.

MAKE THE KENNEL THE SAME WAY AS A RABBIT HUTCH, BUT NO DIVISION IN THE CENTER. YOU WILL NEED TO TAKE OUT THE DIVIDER AND USE THAT AND THE LID TO MAKE THE DOOR AND BEDROOM. AT THE BEDROOM END THE SLATTED WOOD SHOULD FIT TIGHTLY TOGETHER AND THE OTHER END SHOULD HAVE GAPS FOR LIGHT AND AIR.

AT THE BEDROOM END THERE SHOULD BE A VERY SOFT CUSHION FOR THE PUPPY TO SLEEP ON. A BLANKET ALONE WILL NOT KEEP THE PUPPY WARM ENOUGH AT NIGHT. AT THE OTHER END SHOULD BE A SQUARE OF SOD CUT ABOUT THREE INCHES THICK. THIS IS NOT MEANT TO BE USED INSTEAD OF TAKING THE PUPPY OUT, ONLY IN AN EMERGENCY WHEN THE PUPPY CANNOT WAIT.

THE SOD CAN BE WASHED EVERY TWO OR THREE DAYS WITH A HOSE, OR UNDER A SLOW RUNNING TAP, AND DRIED ON A RADIATOR OR IN THE SUN.

YOUR PUPPY MUST ALSO HAVE A BASKET AND A BLANKET. TEACH HIM TO STAY IN THAT WHEN YOU ARE IN THE ROOM. NEVER LEAVE A YOUNG PUPPY OUT OF HIS INDOOR KENNEL WHEN YOU ARE NOT AROUND. REMEMBER TO BUY A BASKET BIG ENOUGH TO ACCOMMODATE HIM WHEN HE GROWS UP.

HOUSE BREAKING TAKES A LOT OF PATIENCE. YOU MUST WATCH YOUR PUPPY FOR ANY SIGNS OF SNIFFING IN AN INTERESTED MANNER, AND IMMEDIATELY PUT HIM OUT ONTO THE GRASS. THIS SHOULD BE DONE ABOUT EVERY TWO HOURS WHEN HE IS TINY, AND AFTER EVERY MEAL.

BE SURE ALWAYS TO TAKE HIM TO THE SAME SPOT. THUS HE SOON CONNECTS THIS SPOT WITH WHAT HE HAS TO DO. GIVE HIM THE WORDS "HURRY UP" WHEN YOU WANT HIM TO PERFORM, AND LOTS OF PRAISE WHEN HE DOES.

IT IS ESSENTIAL TO GET UP EARLY AND TAKE THE PUPPY OUT. IT IS A GOOD THING TO HAVE THE PUPPY WITHIN EARSHOT FOR THE FIRST FEW DAYS, SO HE CAN BE PICKED UP AND TAKEN OUT QUICKLY.

IF YOU HAVE AN APARTMENT AND CANNOT GET NEAR GRASS, USE A TRAY OF SAND IN THE KITCHEN OR BATHROOM - NEVER IN YOUR LIVING ROOM. THE PUPPY MUST NEVER BE ALLOWED TO SOIL IN YOUR OWN ROOMS. NEVER TEACH IT TO USE NEWS-PAPER, OR ONE DAY IT MAY USE THE WALLPAPER.

FEED THE PUPPY ITS WET FOOD NOT LATER THAN 5 P.M. SEE THAT IT HAS RAW CHOPPED MEAT AT 10 P.M. IF POSSIBLE. A PUPPY SLEEPS WELL ON A FULL TUMMY.

PUT THE PUPPY'S INDOOR KENNEL IN A WARM CLOSET WITH THE DOOR OPEN, OR NEAR A RADIATOR. WARMTH IS MOST ESSENTIAL TO CLEANLINESS. NEVER PUT A PUPPY NEAR AN OPEN FLAME. A SPARK MIGHT SET THE KENNEL ON FIRE.

ONCE YOUR PUPPY IS SETTLED FOR THE NIGHT, IGNORE WHINING AND BARKING. IT WILL ONLY LAST A FEW DAYS. BURY YOUR HEAD UNDER THE COVERS AND GO TO HIM ONLY TO SCOLD. NEVER PICK HIM UP AND TAKE HIM TO BED WITH YOU, AS THIS HABIT IS DIFFICULT TO BREAK.

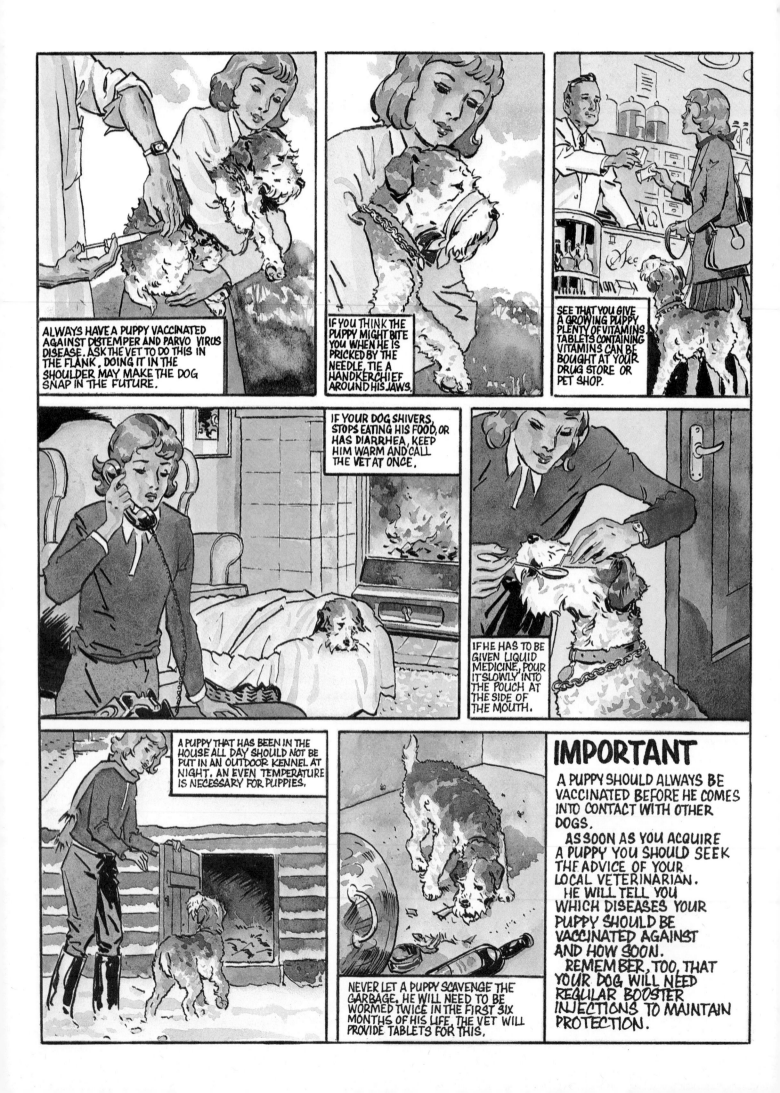

ALWAYS HAVE A PUPPY VACCINATED AGAINST DISTEMPER AND PARVO VIRUS DISEASE. ASK THE VET TO DO THIS IN THE FLANK, DOING IT IN THE SHOULDER MAY MAKE THE DOG SNAP IN THE FUTURE.

IF YOU THINK THE PUPPY MIGHT BITE YOU WHEN HE IS PRICKED BY THE NEEDLE, TIE A HANDKERCHIEF AROUND HIS JAWS.

SEE THAT YOU GIVE A GROWING PUPPY PLENTY OF VITAMINS. TABLETS CONTAINING VITAMINS CAN BE BOUGHT AT YOUR DRUG STORE OR PET SHOP.

IF YOUR DOG SHIVERS, STOPS EATING HIS FOOD, OR HAS DIARRHEA, KEEP HIM WARM AND CALL THE VET AT ONCE.

IF HE HAS TO BE GIVEN LIQUID MEDICINE, POUR IT SLOWLY INTO THE POUCH AT THE SIDE OF THE MOUTH.

A PUPPY THAT HAS BEEN IN THE HOUSE ALL DAY SHOULD NOT BE PUT IN AN OUTDOOR KENNEL AT NIGHT. AN EVEN TEMPERATURE IS NECESSARY FOR PUPPIES.

NEVER LET A PUPPY SCAVENGE THE GARBAGE. HE WILL NEED TO BE WORMED TWICE IN THE FIRST SIX MONTHS OF HIS LIFE. THE VET WILL PROVIDE TABLETS FOR THIS.

IMPORTANT

A PUPPY SHOULD ALWAYS BE VACCINATED BEFORE HE COMES INTO CONTACT WITH OTHER DOGS.

AS SOON AS YOU ACQUIRE A PUPPY YOU SHOULD SEEK THE ADVICE OF YOUR LOCAL VETERINARIAN.

HE WILL TELL YOU WHICH DISEASES YOUR PUPPY SHOULD BE VACCINATED AGAINST AND HOW SOON.

REMEMBER, TOO, THAT YOUR DOG WILL NEED REGULAR BOOSTER INJECTIONS TO MAINTAIN PROTECTION.

LONG-HAIRED DOGS NEED A DAILY GROOMING. IF THE HAIR GETS VERY TANGLED, USE A WIRE BRUSH WITH A RUBBER BASE. A GLOVE BRUSH WORKS FOR SMOOTH-HAIRED DOGS AND A COMB FOR MEDIUM-LENGTH COATS.

DOGS MAY BITE IF YOU PULL THEIR HAIR, AS IT HURTS THEM. SOMETIMES THEY BITE FROM BAD TEMPER ALONE, BUT IF THEY ARE TRAINED WHEN TINY, THIS TROUBLE DOES NOT OCCUR.

WASH YOUR DOG WITH A GOOD DOG SOAP ABOUT SIX TIMES A YEAR TO GET RID OF THE OLD COAT WHICH KEEPS FALLING OUT NATURALLY.

DRY YOUR DOG WELL WITH AN OLD TOWEL IF HE COMES IN WET. IF HE LIVES IN AN OUTDOOR KENNEL, GIVE HIM PLENTY OF STRAW AND HE WILL DRY HIMSELF.

ALL TERRIERS WITH LONG COATS, POODLES, AND SO ON NEED EXPERT TRIMMING AT LEAST TWICE A YEAR. IT IS BEST TO HAVE THIS DONE BY A PROFESSIONAL.

ALL DOGS ARE LIKELY TO PICK UP BUGS IF YOU TAKE THEM FOR COUNTRY WALKS. IF YOU SEE YOUR DOG SCRATCHING A LOT AFTER BATHING HIM, GET SOME DOG'S INSECT POWDER. BE CAREFUL NOT TO GET IT IN HIS EYES.

IF BARE PATCHES APPEAR IN THE DOG'S COAT, IT IS PROBABLY ECZEMA OR MANGE. TAKE HIM TO THE VET AT ONCE.

FEEDING YOUR DOG

THERE ARE MANY SUCCESSFUL METHODS OF FEEDING DOGS. SOME OWNERS PREFER TO USE COMMERCIAL BRANDS OF BISCUITS AND DOG FOOD; OTHERS MAY CHOOSE TO MAKE UP THEIR OWN MENUS. MEAT IN SOME FORM IS ESSENTIAL, AND SO ARE MILK AND WHOLE WHEAT BREAD OR CRACKERS. FISH, LIVER, AND RABBIT ARE ALL GOOD.

ALWAYS HAVE A FEEDING BOWL AND DRINKING BOWL THAT BELONG ONLY TO YOUR DOG. THEN HE WILL LEARN NOT TO TOUCH ANYTHING EXCEPT FROM THESE BOWLS.
GIVE HIM FRESH WATER TWICE A DAY.

NEVER GIVE THE PUPPY POULTRY OR ANYTHING WITH SMALL BONES. IF A BONE GETS STUCK IN THE PUPPY'S THROAT, HOOK YOUR FIRST FINGER IN A CROOKED POSITION AND GENTLY TRY TO DISLODGE IT. IF YOU FAIL, GET A VET QUICKLY.

A SMALL PUPPY NEEDS FOUR MEALS A DAY. START WITH BREAD AND MILK, AND GIVE ALTERNATELY CHOPPED RAW MEAT AND PLAIN MILK (OR PUPPY MEAL IF YOU PREFER). THE MILK SHOULD BE WARMED TO BODY TEMPERATURE (98·6° FAHRENHEIT). USE A THERMOMETER AS ONE'S FINGERS MAY BE UNRELIABLE.

TEACH YOUR DOG AT THREE MONTHS TO REFUSE FOOD FROM STRANGERS. GET THE BUTCHER TO OFFER IT MEAT. THEN BRING YOUR HAND DOWN QUICKLY IN FRONT OF ITS NOSE WITH A SHARP COMMAND "LEAVE." REPEAT AS OFTEN AS NECESSARY. AS SOON AS IT TURNS ITS HEAD AWAY FROM THE MEAT, PRAISE THE DOG AND GIVE IT THE MEAT YOURSELF.

NEVER PICK UP THE PUPPY AND SMACK HIM. HE WILL NOT UNDERSTAND, AND THIS CAN DO NOTHING BUT HARM. PUNISHMENT SHOULD BE BY THE TONE OF YOUR VOICE AND A JERK ON THE COLLAR.

IF GIVEN TO THE DOG BONES SHOULD BE LARGE ONES THAT HE CANNOT CHEW UP. CONTRARY TO COMMON BELIEF, BONES CAN BE VERY BAD FOR A DOG'S DIGESTION. HOWEVER, THEY ARE EXCELLENT TO CUT TEETH ON AND AS PLAYTHINGS.

TRAINING YOUR DOG

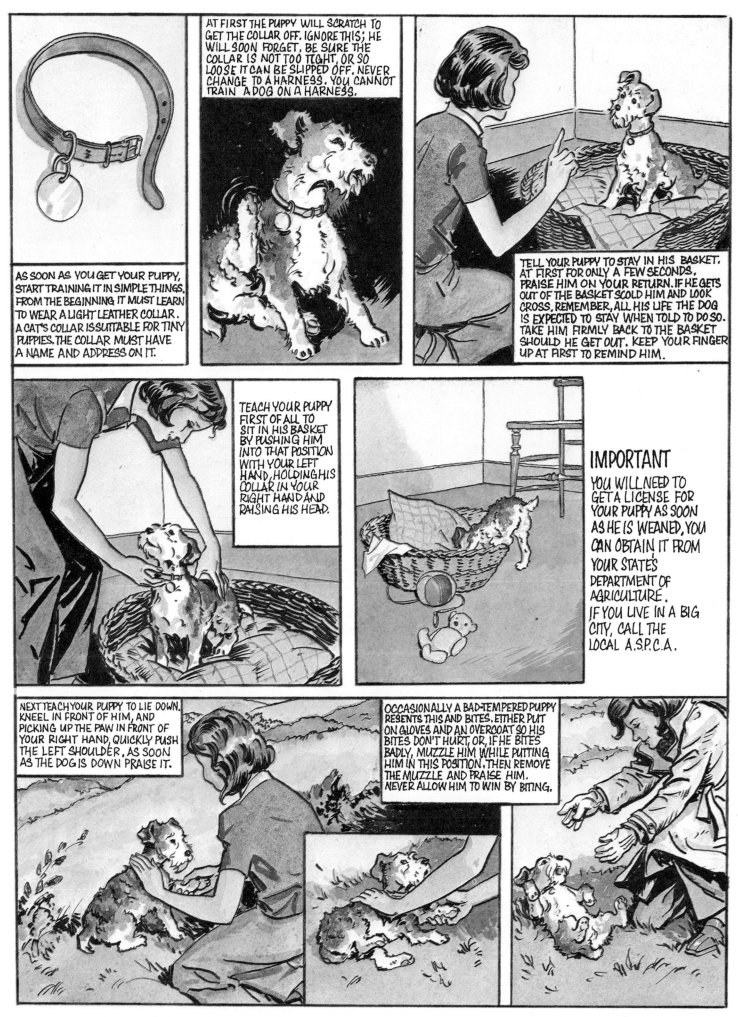

AS SOON AS YOU GET YOUR PUPPY, START TRAINING IT IN SIMPLE THINGS. FROM THE BEGINNING IT MUST LEARN TO WEAR A LIGHT LEATHER COLLAR. A CAT'S COLLAR IS SUITABLE FOR TINY PUPPIES. THE COLLAR MUST HAVE A NAME AND ADDRESS ON IT.

AT FIRST THE PUPPY WILL SCRATCH TO GET THE COLLAR OFF. IGNORE THIS; HE WILL SOON FORGET. BE SURE THE COLLAR IS NOT TOO TIGHT, OR SO LOOSE IT CAN BE SLIPPED OFF. NEVER CHANGE TO A HARNESS. YOU CANNOT TRAIN A DOG ON A HARNESS.

TELL YOUR PUPPY TO STAY IN HIS BASKET. AT FIRST FOR ONLY A FEW SECONDS. PRAISE HIM ON YOUR RETURN. IF HE GETS OUT OF THE BASKET SCOLD HIM AND LOOK CROSS. REMEMBER, ALL HIS LIFE THE DOG IS EXPECTED TO STAY WHEN TOLD TO DO SO. TAKE HIM FIRMLY BACK TO THE BASKET SHOULD HE GET OUT. KEEP YOUR FINGER UP AT FIRST TO REMIND HIM.

TEACH YOUR PUPPY FIRST OF ALL TO SIT IN HIS BASKET BY PUSHING HIM INTO THAT POSITION WITH YOUR LEFT HAND, HOLDING HIS COLLAR IN YOUR RIGHT HAND AND RAISING HIS HEAD.

IMPORTANT

YOU WILL NEED TO GET A LICENSE FOR YOUR PUPPY AS SOON AS HE IS WEANED. YOU CAN OBTAIN IT FROM YOUR STATE'S DEPARTMENT OF AGRICULTURE. IF YOU LIVE IN A BIG CITY, CALL THE LOCAL A.S.P.C.A.

NEXT TEACH YOUR PUPPY TO LIE DOWN. KNEEL IN FRONT OF HIM, AND PICKING UP THE PAW IN FRONT OF YOUR RIGHT HAND, QUICKLY PUSH THE LEFT SHOULDER. AS SOON AS THE DOG IS DOWN PRAISE IT.

OCCASIONALLY A BAD-TEMPERED PUPPY RESENTS THIS AND BITES. EITHER PUT ON GLOVES AND AN OVERCOAT SO HIS BITES DON'T HURT, OR, IF HE BITES BADLY, MUZZLE HIM WHILE PUTTING HIM IN THIS POSITION. THEN REMOVE THE MUZZLE AND PRAISE HIM. NEVER ALLOW HIM TO WIN BY BITING.

WHEN THE PUPPY IS ABOUT FOUR MONTHS OLD YOU CAN START SERIOUS TRAINING. YOU WILL NEED A STRONG LEATHER LEASH ABOUT 1-INCH WIDE; AND BETWEEN THREE AND FOUR FEET LONG, WITH A STRONG CLASP. USE ONLY A TRIGGER CLASP WHEN TRAINING YOUR DOG.

YOU MUST HAVE A CHOKE CHAIN. THIS IS THE KINDER WAY TO TRAIN A DOG, AS IT CLOSES ON THE NECK INSTEAD OF HITTING THE BASE OF THE EARS, AS A LEATHER ONE WOULD DO WHEN JERKED. BUY THE THICK TYPE OF LINK; NEVER THE THIN IN THE MISTAKEN IDEA THAT THE THIN ONE IS LIGHTER AND THEREFORE KINDER. REMEMBER THAT STRING CUTS THE HAND WHEN ROPE WOULDN'T. IT IS THE SAME WITH CHOKE CHAINS, ALTHOUGH NEITHER OF THE CHAINS WOULD ACTUALLY CUT THE DOG.

THERE IS A RIGHT WAY AND A WRONG WAY OF PUTTING ON A CHOKE CHAIN. IF PUT ON THE WRONG WAY IT DOES NOT FREELY RELEASE ITSELF WHEN THE LEASH IS LOOSE; IT STAYS TIGHT ON THE THROAT. WHEN THE DOG IS ON YOUR LEFT SIDE THE LOOSE END OF THE CHAIN SHOULD PULL IN AN UPWARD DIRECTION.

THREAD THE CHAIN BACK THROUGH ITSELF BY HOLDING ONE RING IN THE LEFT HAND AND THE OTHER RING IN THE RIGHT HAND AND DROPPING THE CHAIN THROUGH THE RING HELD IN YOUR LEFT HAND.

NEVER PUT THE CHAIN ON SO IT PULLS IN A DOWNWARD DIRECTION.

ALWAYS TEST THE CHAIN BEFORE STARTING OFF BY RUNNING YOUR HAND IN UNDER THE CHAIN, YOU CAN THEN CHECK THAT IT IS PUT ON THE RIGHT WAY.

IF IT'S ON WRONG, HOLD THE DOG'S SCRUFF IN ONE HAND BEFORE TAKING OFF THE COLLAR TO PUT IT ON CORRECTLY, OR YOU MAY, BY MISTAKE, LET YOUR DOG ESCAPE.

CHOKE CHAINS

TO MEASURE FOR THE CORRECT SIZE, MEASURE OVER THE TOP OF THE DOG'S HEAD, DOWN OVER BOTH EARS AND UNDER THE CHIN, THEN ADD 2 INCHES.

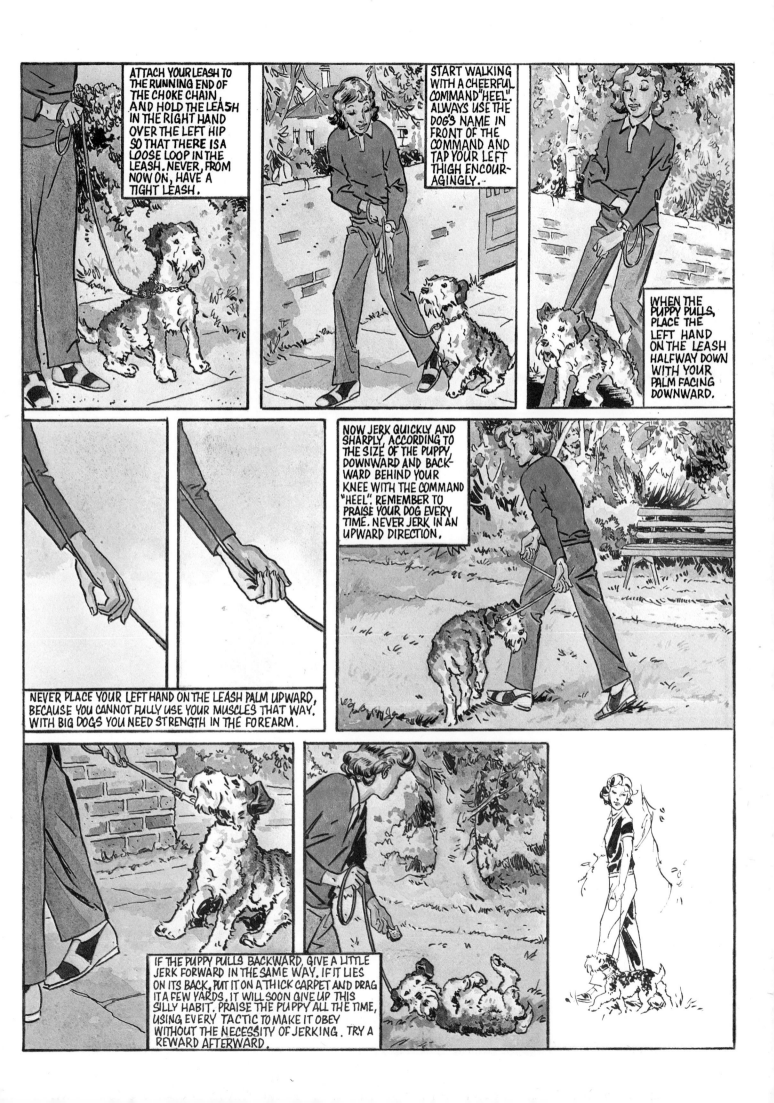

ATTACH YOUR LEASH TO THE RUNNING END OF THE CHOKE CHAIN, AND HOLD THE LEASH IN THE RIGHT HAND OVER THE LEFT HIP SO THAT THERE IS A LOOSE LOOP IN THE LEASH. NEVER, FROM NOW ON, HAVE A TIGHT LEASH.

START WALKING WITH A CHEERFUL COMMAND "HEEL". ALWAYS USE THE DOG'S NAME IN FRONT OF THE COMMAND AND TAP YOUR LEFT THIGH ENCOURAGINGLY...

WHEN THE PUPPY PULLS, PLACE THE LEFT HAND ON THE LEASH HALFWAY DOWN WITH YOUR PALM FACING DOWNWARD.

NEVER PLACE YOUR LEFT HAND ON THE LEASH PALM UPWARD, BECAUSE YOU CANNOT FULLY USE YOUR MUSCLES THAT WAY. WITH BIG DOGS YOU NEED STRENGTH IN THE FOREARM.

NOW JERK QUICKLY AND SHARPLY, ACCORDING TO THE SIZE OF THE PUPPY DOWNWARD AND BACKWARD BEHIND YOUR KNEE WITH THE COMMAND "HEEL". REMEMBER TO PRAISE YOUR DOG EVERY TIME. NEVER JERK IN AN UPWARD DIRECTION.

IF THE PUPPY PULLS BACKWARD, GIVE A LITTLE JERK FORWARD IN THE SAME WAY. IF IT LIES ON ITS BACK, PUT IT ON A THICK CARPET AND DRAG IT A FEW YARDS. IT WILL SOON GIVE UP THIS SILLY HABIT. PRAISE THE PUPPY ALL THE TIME, USING EVERY TACTIC TO MAKE IT OBEY WITHOUT THE NECESSITY OF JERKING. TRY A REWARD AFTERWARD.

AT THE END OF EVERY EXERCISE, PRAISE YOUR DOG BY PUTTING THE LEFT HAND UNDER THE DOG'S CHIN AND RAISING HIS HEAD SO HE CAN SEE YOUR FACE; THEN SCRATCH HIS CHEST WITH THE RIGHT HAND.

A DOG OBEYS ITS OWNER FOR TWO REASONS, LOVE AND RESPECT. THE RESPECT YOU GAIN BY FIRM COMMANDS; THE LOVE, BY THE TONE OF THE VOICE, THE SMILE ON YOUR LIPS AND IN YOUR EYES, AND THE LOVING THOUGHTS YOU SEND OUT BY TELEPATHY.

ALWAYS APPROACH A DOG WITH THE PALM FACING UPWARD, AND THE ARM HELD LOW. APPROACH WITH CONFIDENCE, OR THE DOG WILL MISTRUST YOU. LET HIM HAVE A SHORT SNIFF AT YOU; THEN SCRATCH HIS CHEST.

NEVER APPROACH WITH HAND HELD HIGH AS IF TO TOUCH ITS HEAD. IT MAY THINK YOU ARE GOING TO CATCH HOLD OF ITS COLLAR AND IT MAY BITE.

NEVER TOUCH OTHER PEOPLE'S DOGS IN THE STREET WITHOUT FIRST ASKING PERMISSION. LET DOGS ALONE THAT ARE LEFT SITTING OUTSIDE SHOPS. TRAINED DOGS SHOULD NEVER BE DISTURBED OR THEY MAY FORGET THEIR TRAINING AND RUN OFF. YOU MAY LOVE DOGS, BUT ALL DOGS MAY NOT LOVE YOU.

IF YOU HAVE A DOG WITH YOU NEVER LET IT SNIFF ANYONE ELSE'S DOG. IT MAY PICK UP AN INFECTION, OR GET BITTEN BY THE OTHER DOG. BUT BY ALL MEANS LET YOUR DOG PLAY WITH OTHER DOGS WHEN THEIR OWNERS ALLOW IT.

NEVER GIVE FOOD TO ANYONE ELSE'S DOG. IT MAY HAVE INDIGESTION WHICH YOUR TIDBIT MAY MAKE WORSE.

MAKE YOUR DOG SIT EVERY TIME YOU STOP. TO DO THIS, RAISE YOUR RIGHT HAND HOLDING THE LEASH UP AND OVER YOUR RIGHT HIP, SIMULTANEOUSLY PUSH THE PUPPY DOWN, BY PLACING YOUR LEFT HAND ON HIS BACK WITH THE INDEX FINGER IN FRONT OF HIS THIGH-BONE AND THE REST OF THE FINGERS SPREAD OVER HIS BACK, THUMB TOWARD YOUR OWN LEG, SCOOP HIM IN CLOSE TO YOU.

NEVER ALLOW YOUR DOG ANYWHERE OUTSIDE YOUR OWN PROPERTY BY ITSELF. HOWEVER WELL TRAINED IT MAY BE, ALWAY KEEP IT ON THE LEASH IN THE STREET. IF YOU DON'T IT MAY SEE ANOTHER DOG OR BE ATTACKED UNEXPECTEDLY AND SWERVE INTO THE ROAD. THOUSANDS OF ACCIDENTS A YEAR ARE CAUSED BY UNCONTROLLED DOGS ON THE HIGHWAY.

IF HE LIES DOWN INSTEAD OF SITTING, YOUR RIGHT HAND, HOLDING THE LEASH, IS NOT HIGH ENOUGH. HIS HEAD SHOULD BE GENTLY BUT FIRMLY KEPT IN A POSITION THAT WILL MAKE IT IMPOSSIBLE FOR HIM TO LIE DOWN. USE THE CHOKE CHAIN TO LIFT HIM, MAKING SURE THE RUNNING END IS UNDER THE CHIN. PRAISE HIM EVERY TIME HE SITS.

NEVER PUT YOUR HAND ON HIS BACK THE WRONG WAY AROUND. THIS WILL BE MUCH SLOWER AND LESS EFFECTIVE.

NEVER LIFT A DOG BY THE CHOKE CHAIN WITH THE RUNNING END ON TOP OF HIS NECK. THE UNDERNEATH OF A DOG'S THROAT IS DELICATE AND IT MIGHT HURT HIM.

SPENCE & COY

BEFORE CROSSING THE STREET ALWAYS MAKE YOUR DOG SIT, AND THEN LOOK BOTH WAYS. TRAINED DOGS ARE SAFE DOGS.

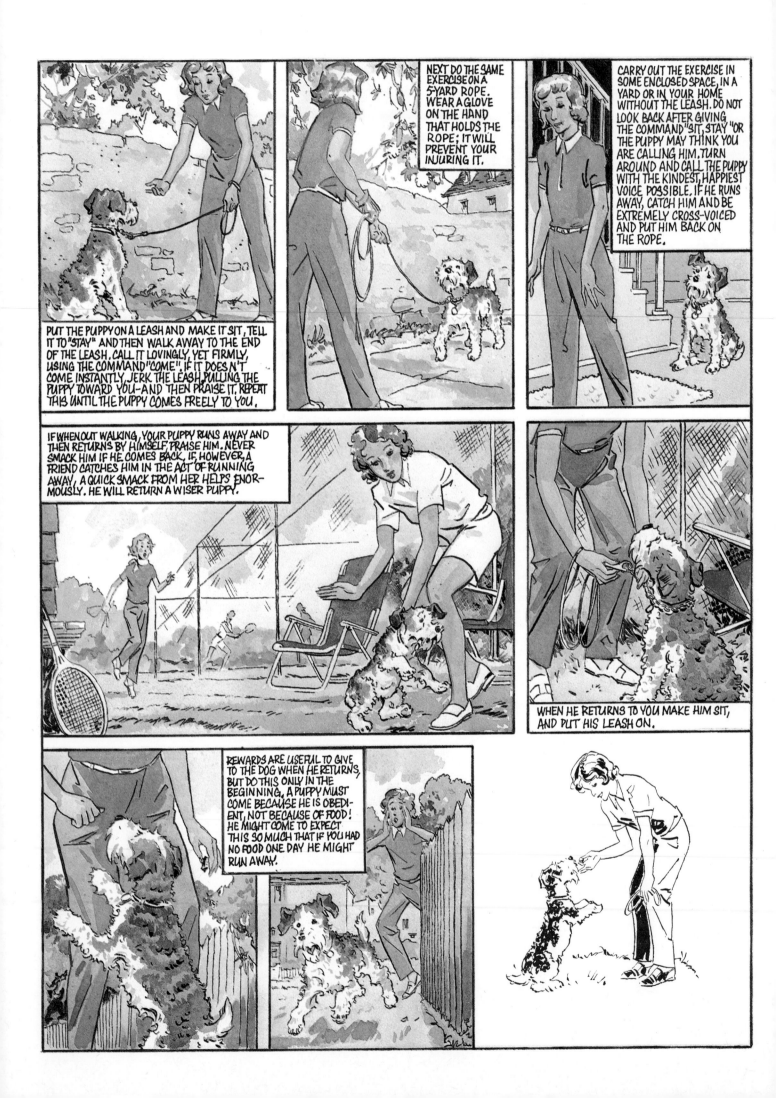

NEXT DO THE SAME EXERCISE ON A 5-YARD ROPE. WEAR A GLOVE ON THE HAND THAT HOLDS THE ROPE; IT WILL PREVENT YOUR INJURING IT.

CARRY OUT THE EXERCISE IN SOME ENCLOSED SPACE, IN A YARD OR IN YOUR HOME WITHOUT THE LEASH. DO NOT LOOK BACK AFTER GIVING THE COMMAND "SIT, STAY "OR THE PUPPY MAY THINK YOU ARE CALLING HIM. TURN AROUND AND CALL THE PUPPY WITH THE KINDEST, HAPPIEST VOICE POSSIBLE. IF HE RUNS AWAY, CATCH HIM AND BE EXTREMELY CROSS-VOICED AND PUT HIM BACK ON THE ROPE.

PUT THE PUPPY ON A LEASH AND MAKE IT SIT, TELL IT TO "STAY" AND THEN WALK AWAY TO THE END OF THE LEASH. CALL IT LOVINGLY, YET FIRMLY, USING THE COMMAND "COME". IF IT DOESN'T COME INSTANTLY, JERK THE LEASH PULLING THE PUPPY TOWARD YOU-AND THEN PRAISE IT. REPEAT THIS UNTIL THE PUPPY COMES FREELY TO YOU.

IF WHEN OUT WALKING, YOUR PUPPY RUNS AWAY AND THEN RETURNS BY HIMSELF, PRAISE HIM. NEVER SMACK HIM IF HE COMES BACK. IF HOWEVER A FRIEND CATCHES HIM IN THE ACT OF RUNNING AWAY, A QUICK SMACK FROM HER HELPS ENORMOUSLY. HE WILL RETURN A WISER PUPPY.

WHEN HE RETURNS TO YOU MAKE HIM SIT, AND PUT HIS LEASH ON.

REWARDS ARE USEFUL TO GIVE TO THE DOG WHEN HE RETURNS, BUT DO THIS ONLY IN THE BEGINNING. A PUPPY MUST COME BECAUSE HE IS OBEDIENT, NOT BECAUSE OF FOOD! HE MIGHT COME TO EXPECT THIS SO MUCH THAT IF YOU HAD NO FOOD ONE DAY HE MIGHT RUN AWAY.

ALL EXERCISES END IN THE SAME WAY. THE DOG GOES AROUND TO THE LEFT-HAND SIDE OF ITS OWNER, WHERE IT IS PRAISED FOR A JOB WELL DONE. TO TEACH THIS, PUT YOUR DOG ON THE LEASH HELD IN THE RIGHT HAND. HOLD THE LEASH AND GENTLY JERK THE DOG, WITH YOUR HAND AWAY FROM YOUR BODY.

AS THE DOG GETS TO YOUR RIGHT-HAND SIDE, PASS THE LEASH TO YOUR LEFT HAND BEHIND YOU.

LET GO OF THE LEASH WITH YOUR RIGHT HAND AND TURN YOUR HEAD TO THE LEFT TO ENCOURAGE THE DOG TO COME TO YOU.

AS THE DOG COMES INTO THE CORRECT POSITION ON YOUR LEFT SIDE, TAKE THE LEASH BACK INTO THE RIGHT HAND, RAISE IT OVER YOUR RIGHT HIP, PUSH THE DOG TO "SIT". PRAISE HIM.

AFTER EVERY EXERCISE PLAY WITH YOUR DOG,

NEXT TRY THIS OFF THE LEASH, TAP YOUR RIGHT THIGH AT FIRST, THEN YOUR LEFT SIDE, BENDING DOWN SLIGHTLY, TO HELP YOUR DOG SEE YOUR FACE, ENCOURAGE HIM WITH YOUR VOICE TOO. A LOT DEPENDS ON HOW NICE YOU SOUND.

IF IT IS ABSOLUTELY NECESSARY GIVE HIM A REWARD FIRST.

TEACHING YOUR DOG TO LIE DOWN AND STAY DOWN IS THE MOST DIFFICULT EXERCISE OF ALL.

TO GET A DOG TO LIE DOWN QUICKLY, PLACE YOUR RIGHT HAND ON THE RUNNING END OF THE CHOKE CHAIN AND QUICKLY PULL HIS HEAD TO THE GROUND. MAKE SURE THE RUNNING END IS UNDER HIS CHIN. THEN GIVE A QUICK PUSH WITH LEFT HAND ON HIS BACK. NEVER LET HIM SIT FIRST. GIVE FIRM COMMAND "DOWN".

WHEN THE DOG IS DOWN, WALK TO THE END OF THE LEASH AND THEN AROUND THE DOG. REPEAT THE WORDS "DOWN-STAY!" AS OFTEN AS NECESSARY.

COME BACK TO YOUR DOG AND STAND AT HIS SIDE FOR A MOMENT AND WALK OFF AGAIN. IF HE GETS UP, PUT HIM DOWN AGAIN, REPEATING COMMAND "DOWN-STAY!" THE NEXT TIME BACK, PRAISE HIM.

NEXT DROP YOUR LEASH AND REPEAT THE EXERCISE. THEN ASK A FRIEND TO WALK HER DOG PAST YOURS. IF IT ATTEMPTS TO MOVE, SAY, "NAUGHTY DOG, DOWN!" VERY CROSSLY. WHEN IT STAYS PUT, PRAISE YOUR DOG.

NOW GET LOTS OF FRIENDS TO RUN PAST THE PUPPY, CLAPPING THEIR HANDS AND OCCASIONALLY DROPPING A BOOK A FEW FEET FROM IT. THIS WILL ACCUSTOM IT TO NOISE.

WHEN YOUR DOG IS USED TO THIS, PUT HIM DOWN AND GO OUT OF SIGHT INTO YOUR HOUSE. WATCH THE DOG FROM THE WINDOW AND IF HE MOVES, SHOUT "DOWN!" BY THIS TIME HE SHOULD DROP EVEN THOUGH HE CAN'T SEE YOU.

A DOG JUMPS UP TO BE NEAR YOUR FACE-DOGS LOVE HUMAN FACES. IF POSSIBLE, ALWAYS GET DOWN ON ONE KNEE TO GREET YOUR DOG.

WHEN YOUR DOG JUMPS UP, CATCH HIM BY THE RUNNING END OF THE CHOKE CHAIN AND WITH A SCOLDING VOICE, SAY "NAUGHTY DOG, SIT". THEN PULL HIM SHARPLY TO THE SIT.

NEVER HIT A DOG WITH A NEWSPAPER WHEN HE JUMPS UP. IT IS AN INEFFECTIVE METHOD OF PUNISHING A DOG.

IF YOUR DOG STILL INSISTS ON JUMPING UP, TAP HIM ON THE NOSE WITH YOUR OPEN PALM WHEN HE DOES IT. THIS WILL BE SURE TO CURE HIM, BUT TRY EVERYTHING ELSE FIRST.

SOME DOGS MAY CATCH HOLD OF YOUR CLOTHING TO ATTRACT YOUR ATTENTION. THIS IS MOSTLY DONE OUT OF AFFECTION, BUT IT IS A NUISANCE.

TO CURE THIS, FILL A SMALL JUG WITH WATER, POUR A LITTLE OVER THE DOG'S HEAD EVERY TIME HE CATCHES HOLD OF YOUR CLOTHING. HE WILL SOON GIVE IT UP.

AFTER EVERY CORRECTION, PET YOUR DOG TO SHOW HIM THAT IT IS HIS ACTIONS ONLY THAT ARE AT FAULT.

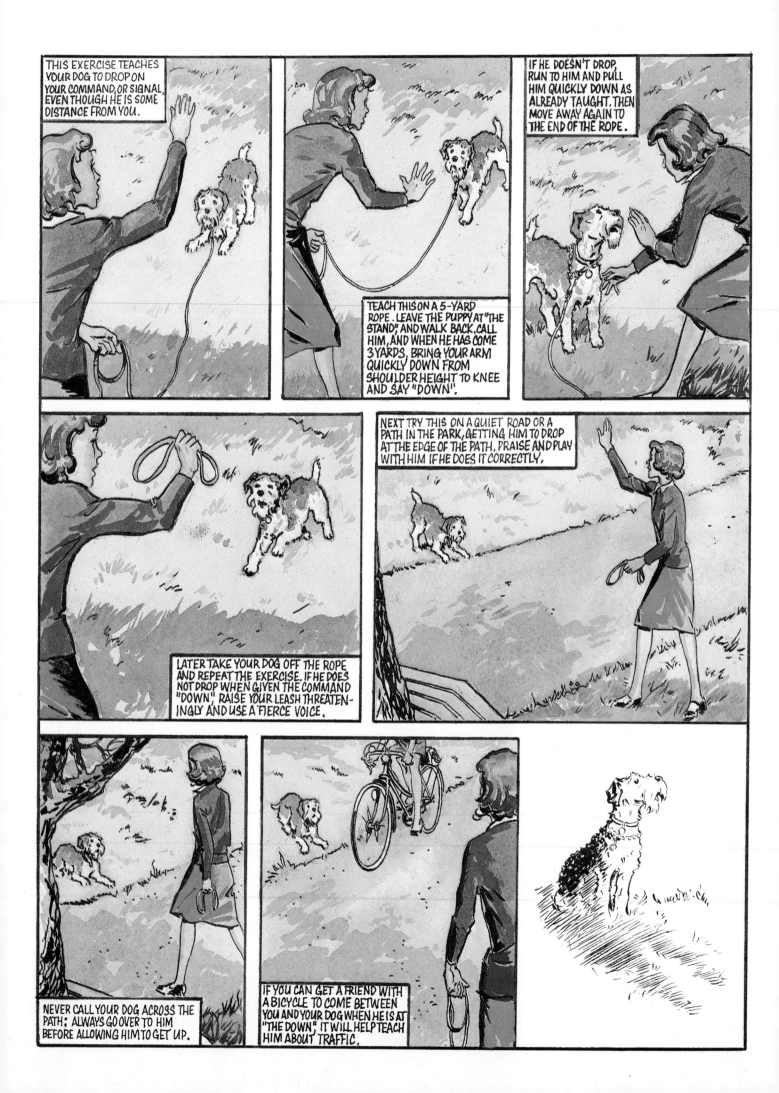

THIS EXERCISE TEACHES YOUR DOG TO DROP ON YOUR COMMAND, OR SIGNAL, EVEN THOUGH HE IS SOME DISTANCE FROM YOU.

TEACH THIS ON A 5-YARD ROPE. LEAVE THE PUPPY AT "THE STAND", AND WALK BACK. CALL HIM, AND WHEN HE HAS COME 3 YARDS, BRING YOUR ARM QUICKLY DOWN FROM SHOULDER HEIGHT TO KNEE AND SAY "DOWN".

IF HE DOESN'T DROP, RUN TO HIM AND PULL HIM QUICKLY DOWN AS ALREADY TAUGHT. THEN MOVE AWAY AGAIN TO THE END OF THE ROPE.

LATER TAKE YOUR DOG OFF THE ROPE AND REPEAT THE EXERCISE. IF HE DOES NOT DROP WHEN GIVEN THE COMMAND "DOWN", RAISE YOUR LEASH THREATENINGLY AND USE A FIERCE VOICE.

NEXT TRY THIS ON A QUIET ROAD OR A PATH IN THE PARK, GETTING HIM TO DROP AT THE EDGE OF THE PATH. PRAISE AND PLAY WITH HIM IF HE DOES IT CORRECTLY.

NEVER CALL YOUR DOG ACROSS THE PATH; ALWAYS GO OVER TO HIM BEFORE ALLOWING HIM TO GET UP.

IF YOU CAN GET A FRIEND WITH A BICYCLE TO COME BETWEEN YOU AND YOUR DOG WHEN HE IS AT "THE DOWN" IT WILL HELP TEACH HIM ABOUT TRAFFIC.

GENERAL BEHAVIOR

BAD HABITS CONTRACTED BY DOGS ARE: BITING DELIVERY PEOPLE; CHASING LIVESTOCK; KILLING CHICKENS AND CHEWING FURNITURE.

INSTEAD OF THE WIRE PLAYGROUND, YOU CAN TIE HIM, BY HIS CHAIN, TO A LONG WIRE, FIXED FIRMLY AT BOTH ENDS. THIS ALLOWS HIM TO RUN UP AND DOWN FREELY.

THE CURE FOR BITING DELIVERY PEOPLE IS SIMPLE: KEEP YOUR DOG UNDER CONTROL AT ALL TIMES. IF HE BITES, MAKE A PLAYGROUND BEHIND WIRE IN THE YARD FOR HIM. NEVER ALLOW HIM UNCONTROLLED FREEDOM WHERE STRANGERS CAN BE EXPECTED TO PASS.

NEVER LET HIM FREE AMONG LIVESTOCK ON A FARM. IF HE DOESN'T COME WHEN CALLED, KEEP HIM ON A LONG ROPE.

IF HE KILLS CHICKENS PUT HIM ON A LONG ROPE, AND WHILE YOU HAVE HIM FIRMLY ON THE ROPE, THROW THE DEAD CHICKEN AWAY. HE WILL GO AFTER IT, SO DRAG HIM TO YOU. PICK UP THE CHICKEN AND FLAP IT HARD ALL OVER HIM. HE WILL BE FRIGHTENED OF CHICKENS FROM THEN ON.

TEACH YOUR DOG TO LOVE CATS BY HOLDING THE PUPPY'S COLLAR AND STROKING THE CAT AT THE SAME TIME. PROVIDED THE CAT IS USED TO DOGS, THEY WILL SOON MAKE FRIENDS.

KEEP YOUR PUPPY IN AN INDOOR KENNEL WHEN YOU ARE NOT WITH HIM SO HE NEVER LEARNS TO CHEW FURNITURE. IF HE DOES CHEW IT, SHOW HIM WHAT HE HAS DONE, SCOLD HIM SEVERELY, AND PUT HIM IN HIS KENNEL.

HINTS FOR THE DOG SHOW

IF YOU WANT TO SHOW YOUR DOG IN THE BEAUTY SHOW RING, TRAIN HIM TO STAND CORRECTLY ON A LOOSE LEASH. IF HE SITS, LIFT HIM BY PLACING BOTH HANDS OVER HIS BACK, FINGERS TIGHT INTO HIS THIGHS, AND SET HIM FIRMLY ON HIS FEET WITH THE COMMAND "STAND".

NEXT TRAIN HIM TO TROT BESIDE YOU ON A LOOSE LEASH. IF HE JUMPS UP JERK HIM SHARPLY DOWN AND GIVE THE COMMAND "TROT".

TRAIN HIM TO STAND STILL WHILE THE JUDGE RUNS HIS HANDS ALL OVER HIM. GET YOUR FRIENDS TO BE JUDGES, GIVE HIM THE COMMAND "STAND STAY". PRAISE HIM AS SOON AS THE EXAMINATION IS FINISHED.

TEACH HIM TO HAVE HIS MOUTH OPENED BY YOU SO THAT THE "BITE" CAN BE EXAMINED. IT IS NECESSARY ONLY TO SHOW HIS FRONT TEETH. ALWAYS PUT ONE HAND OVER THE TOP OF THE MUZZLE AND ONE UNDERNEATH THE JAW AND LIFT THE LIPS BACK.

ATTRACT YOUR DOG'S ATTENTION WHILE THE JUDGE IS LOOKING AT HIM BY HOLDING A TIDBIT OR HIS FAVORITE TOY IN YOUR HAND.

DON'T LET YOUR DOG SNIFF ANOTHER IN THE RING, YOU MIGHT SPOIL THAT DOG'S CHANCES OF WINNING AND YOU'D BE UNPOPULAR!

NEVER SPEAK TO THE JUDGE UNLESS HE SPEAKS TO YOU -OTHERWISE YOU MAY BE DISQUALIFIED.

JUDGE

JUD

ABOUT THE AUTHOR

BARBARA WOODHOUSE, "the lady with the dogs," is already familiar to millions of Americans through the publication of her best-selling book, NO BAD DOGS, and her frequent appearances on such national television shows as "60 Minutes," "The Tonight Show," "Phil Donahue," "Merv Griffin," "Good Morning America," "Hour Magazine," and "P.M. Magazine." Born in Dublin in 1910 and raised in Oxford, England, Barbara Woodhouse spent three years during the 1930's on a cattle ranch in Argentina where her extraordinary gift with animals enabled her to break hundreds of wild horses. Married to Dr. Michael Woodhouse on her return to England, she has run a farm, bred and broken horses, and trained 17,000 dogs on her famous weekend courses which teach perfect obedience to basic commands in only six and a half hours. Her Great Danes, Juno and Junia, made more than 100 film and TV appearances, and her own films, records, television series and books have earned her international fame. For information concerning the items Barbara Woodhouse uses when training dogs, send a self-addressed, stamped envelope with your inquiry to JMD Professional Services, P.O. Box 480392, Los Angeles, California 90048.